W9-CHZ-678

YOUR LAND
AND
MY LAND

We Visit
PERU

Bonnie

Hinman

Mitchell Lane
PUBLISHERS
P.O. Box 196
Hockessin, Delaware 19707

YOUR LAND
AND
MY LAND

Brazil
Chile
Colombia
Cuba
Dominican Republic
Mexico
Panama
Peru
Puerto Rico
Venezuela

We Visit

PERU

Printing   1   2   3   4   5   6   7   8   9

Library of Congress Cataloging-in-Publication Data
Hinman, Bonnie.
   We visit Peru/by Bonnie Hinman.
        p. cm. — (Your land and my land)
   Includes bibliographical references and index.
   ISBN 978-1-58415-886-8 (library bound)
   1. Peru—Juvenile literature. I. Title.
   F3408.5.H56 2010
   985—dc22
                                                    2010026966

PUBLISHER'S NOTE: This story is based on the author's extensive research, which she believes to be accurate. Documentation of this research is on page 61.

   The Internet sites referenced herein were active as of the publication date. Due to the fleeting nature of some web sites, we cannot guarantee they will all

Contents

Introduction 6
1 Peru's Beginnings 9
 Facts at a Glance 13
 Where in the World Is Peru? 14
 Hiram Bingham, Explorer 17
2 Who's in Charge? 19
3 Extreme Geography 25
4 Peru's People 31
5 Jobs in Peru 37
6 Sports, Music, and Food 43
7 Famous Peruvians 47
8 Visiting Peru 53
Peruvian Recipe: *Tacu Tacu* 58
Peruvian Craft: Inca Water Jar Replica 59
Timeline 60
Further Reading 61
 Books 61
 Works Consulted 61
 On the Internet 61
Glossary 62
Index 63

Introduction

South of the United States lies a vast area known as Latin America. Covering Mexico, parts of the Caribbean, and Central and South America, the languages spoken there were derived from Latin: Spanish, Portuguese, and French. These languages were introduced when explorers from Europe sailed across the Atlantic and claimed the land for their native countries. But the rich histories of Latin American countries began well before Europeans arrived.

Ask about the wonders of Peru, and you will probably hear of "lost cities" that were thriving before the Europeans arrived, such as Machu Picchu, one of the homes of the Inca people. You might also find out about the Moche pyramids and the Nazca Lines, evidence that the indigenous people of Peru were advanced civilizations.

Peru's geography allowed many different cultures to develop in isolation from the others. They began to mix when the Inca moved tribes they had conquered to different parts of their kingdom, where they would cause less trouble.

The Spanish and Peruvian cultures began mixing almost from the time Francisco Pizarro and his conquistadores arrived in Peru in April 1528. Cuzco, which sits above the ruins of Machu Picchu, is a combination of Spanish and Inca historical sites. Africans were brought in as slaves during the Spanish rule, and by the mid-nineteenth century, plantation and railroad workers arrived from China and Japan. Italian, Palestinian, German, and Austrian immigrants arrived soon after. The mixing of all these people and cultures underlies almost every aspect of Peruvian life. The food of Peru is internationally known for its variety and superb flavors. The music, dance, and literature also reflect the cultural mix.

LATIN AMERICA

Peru welcomes travelers and provides experiences that can't be found anywhere else in the world.

Huge sand dunes west of the city of Ica in southern Peru are part of the Ica Desert. The dunes are the perfect place for sandboarding and dune buggy driving. Marine fossil hunters also come here because this area was part of the ocean over two million years ago.

Chapter 1

Peru's Beginnings

Up until the 1800s, historians and other observers thought that the Inca civilization, with its architectural and engineering achievements, was the beginning of Peruvian culture. Nineteenth-century archaeologists began to make discoveries on Peru's coasts and in its highlands that proved historians wrong.

The earliest traces of people living in Peru—or in South America, for that matter—were found in Pikimachay (Flea Cave) near Ayacucho in the central highlands. These people were nomadic cave dwellers. Tools and bones found in the cave were dated to 12,000 BCE.

The earliest Peruvians who settled in communities lived along the Pacific coast in river valleys starting around 3000 BCE, which places them at least 4000 years before the Inca ruled the land in the 1400s. Residents lived in fishing villages along the Pacific coast. Eventually they moved inland, where they grew vegetables and developed pottery and weaving.

The ruins of Caral on the coast north of Lima are said to be from the earliest known urban center in the Americas. Around 2800 BCE, an estimated 3,000 people lived there among six pyramids arranged around a central courtyard. The people raised cotton, peanuts, and beans, and fished in the ocean. Over 30 bone flutes carved with monkey designs found there suggest that the residents had music. Because there were no monkeys on the coast, they may have traded with people as far away as the Amazon Basin.

Monuments built with stone blocks appeared by 1800 BCE; stone platforms, sunken courtyards, and temples came soon after. Early cultures rose and fell, each making advances in weaving, pottery, and metalworking techniques.

Several of the early cultures left behind evidence of their advances, including the Chavín people. Chavín de Huántar was the capital of the Chavín culture, which spread over the highlands from 900 to 200 BCE. Located east of Huaraz, the site is open to tourists and includes a sunken plaza ringed with carvings of pumas and priests. There is a U-shaped stone temple and underground chambers. The Chavín culture was the first to spread widely across Peru, and it influenced many of the cultures that followed.

On the southern desert coast of Peru, a visitor can see the famous Nazca Lines. The Nazca etched giant images of birds, whales, insects, and other animals into the surface of the San José desert starting around 200 BCE. The desert was covered with a thin layer of manganese and iron oxides. Called desert varnish, this top layer could be removed to reveal a lighter surface below. Rocks were piled along the lines to make them more visible.

The Moche people of the northern coastal valley of Trujillo were famed for their ceramics. They also built irrigation canals and field systems that stretched for miles, connecting neighboring valleys. The system ensured a steady supply of vegetables such as squash, peppers, and beans. Their rise to power began around 100 CE and lasted until 800 CE. They were also accomplished metalsmiths, perfecting a method to gild copper objects.

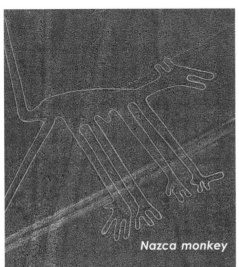

Nazca monkey

An important discovery about the Moche Empire was the tomb of the Lord of Sipán, found in 1987 by Peruvian archaeologist

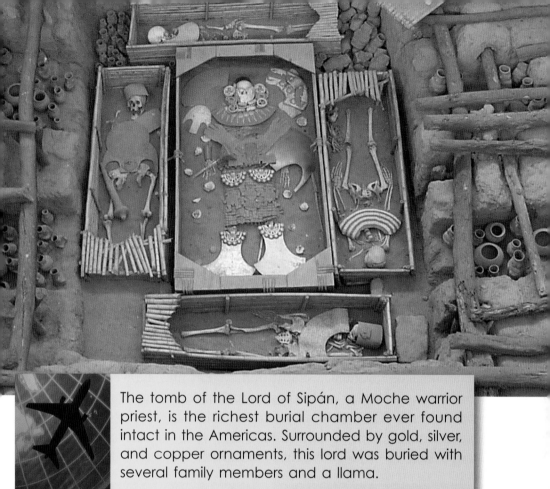

The tomb of the Lord of Sipán, a Moche warrior priest, is the richest burial chamber ever found intact in the Americas. Surrounded by gold, silver, and copper ornaments, this lord was buried with several family members and a llama.

Walter Alva. Unlike most ancient tombs, this one had not been disturbed by grave robbers. The Lord of Sipán, who lived between 200 and 300 CE, was buried with elaborate gold ornaments and the bodies of seven sacrificial victims.

The tomb is near the northern city of Chiclayo and is open to visitors. The treasures that were removed from the tomb are located in the Museo Tumbas Reales de Sipán, north of Chiclayo in Lambayeque.

FYI FACT:

When an Inca emperor died, his body was mummified and kept in his former home. His household attended to the mummy as if it were still royalty. They set out food and drink daily for the mummy and occasionally paraded it around Cuzco during festivals.

Another culture became important about the time the Moche declined, and the remnants of that culture are in the same area as those of the Moche Empire. The Sicán culture built two capitals, one after another. The first was built around 800 CE at Batán Grande, located northeast of Chiclayo. Batán Grande was mysteriously abandoned around 1050 CE, and Tucumé was built north of Chiclayo. Both sites had complexes of adobe pyramids and can be visited by tourists. The elaborate burial sites left by the Sicáns told of a rich and powerful people. The artifacts discovered in the tombs are in the Museo Nacional Sicán in Ferreñafe.

Another culture gained power in the southern part of Peru near Lake Titicaca during the first millennium. Tiahuanaco was the highest urban settlement of the time. At over 12,000 feet above sea level, the Tiahuanacos invented a cultivation system that allowed them to produce a much higher yield on a parcel of land than might commonly be expected. They used a system of canals and raised fields. Tiahuanaco flourished until almost 1000 CE when climate change made it impossible to produce enough food for the people.

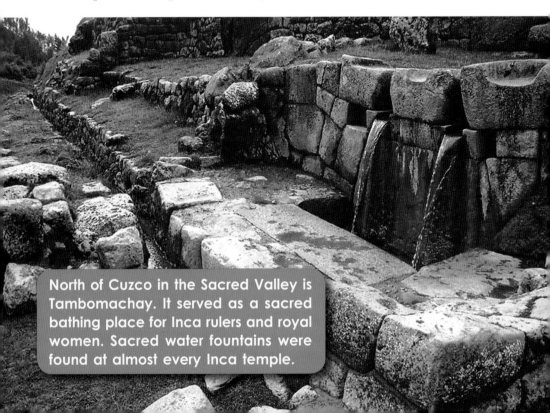

North of Cuzco in the Sacred Valley is Tambomachay. It served as a sacred bathing place for Inca rulers and royal women. Sacred water fountains were found at almost every Inca temple.

PERU FACTS AT A GLANCE

Andean Cock-of-the-Rock

Official Country Name: Republic of Peru
Land Area: 795,351 square miles (1,279,996 square kilometers)
Size comparison: Slightly smaller than Alaska
Population: 29,907,003 (July 2010 estimate)
Capital: Lima
Other large cities: Arequipa, Trujillo
Religions: Roman Catholicism, Evangelism, other
Exports: copper, gold, zinc, crude petroleum and petroleum products, coffee, potatoes, asparagus, textiles, fishmeal
Highest Point: Mount Huascarán—22,200 feet (6,768 meters)
Lowest Point: Pacific Ocean—sea level
Average temperature: 66°F (19°C) to 80°F (27°C)
Currency: Nuevo sol (PEN)
Official languages: Spanish and Quechua
Government: Constitutional Republic
Administrative divisions: 25 departments subdivided into 180 provinces and 1,747 districts
Flag: The Peruvian flag, designed by José de San Martín of Argentina, was adopted on February 25, 1825. The red stripes stand for the blood spilled for freedom. The white stripe stands for peace. The coat of arms has a vicuña and a cinchona tree to represent the animals and plants of Peru. It also has a yellow cornucopia with coins spilling out to represent prosperity.
National flower: Cantuta (*Cantua buxifolia*)
National bird: Andean Cock-of-the-Rock

Sources: *CIA World Factbook,* Peru; U.S. Department of State: Peru

WHERE IN THE WORLD IS PERU?

Colombia

Ecuador

Tumbes

Talara

Piura

Arica

Napo River

Tigre

Iquitos

Amazon River

Maranon River

PERU

Chiclayo

Trujillo   Chachapoyas

Tarapoto

Pucallpa

Brazil

Chimbote

Ucayali River

Huaraz

Huanuco

Pacific
Ocean   Callao

Lima   Huancayo

Ayacucho   Machu Picchu

Cuzco

Puerto Maldonado

Ica   Nazca

Andes
Mtns.

Lake
Titicaca

Where in the World

Arequipa

Tacna

Bolivia

Chile

Andes Mtns.

Peru is located on the western side of South America bordering the Pacific Ocean. It shares borders with Ecuador, Colombia, Brazil, Bolivia, and Chile. It also shares Lake Titicaca with Bolivia—the border between the two countries divides the lake near the middle.

Descended from people who had lived in the valley of Cuzco, the Inca did not become known as a distinct people until around 1200 CE. They remained local until 1438 when Pachacutec Inca Yupanqui, the ninth leader of the Inca, emerged; after that, they gradually extended their influence. Pachacutec marched through the Andes, conquering other tribes until a great empire stretched the length of Peru.

Chan Chan, the ancient capitol of the Chimú civilization, was once home to as many as 60,000 people. The Chimú left no written records, but the eroded buildings and walls have carvings of fish, birds, fishing nets, and moons.

Yet another ancient culture was located farther south along the Pacific coast. The Chimú civilization emerged around 900 CE from north of present-day Lima to Tumbes. The Chimú built a magnificent city called Chan Chan, which is said to be the largest adobe city ever constructed. Built about 1300 CE, Chan Chan was elaborately sculpted and painted with complex networks of courtyards, passages, terraces, gardens, palaces, and homes.

Chan Chan is considered one of the most important archaeological sites in Peru. Visitors can tour the ruins near Trujillo along with three other Chimú sites. The Chimú people finally fell to the Inca around 1464, not long before the Spanish arrived in Peru.

The Inca used a system of labor tax called *mita* to build roads and government buildings, repair bridges, and raise food crops. Inca citizens did not pay taxes. They worked for the government in whatever capacity the leaders desired, paying their taxes in labor. Historians believe that this system allowed the Inca Empire to come as close to eliminating hunger as any nation ever has.

For all their power and glory, the Inca Empire lasted little longer than 100 years. The empire began to fall apart when emperor Huayna Capac died in 1525 without naming a successor. Two of his sons and their supporters fought a bitter civil war before Atahualpa took the throne in 1532. He became emperor only months before Spanish explorer Francisco Pizarro arrived in Peru. When Pizarro arrived, the bloody conquest of the Inca began.

The Inca did not immediately recognize Pizarro and his men as enemies. They saw the conquistadores as interesting strangers and gave them a royal welcome. The devious Pizarro promised friendship but took Atahualpa captive and eventually had him killed. The Inca fought bravely against Pizarro, but they were doomed. Weakened by disease and civil war, the Inca finally succumbed to the horses, superior weapons, and steel armor of the Spanish.

During their colonial rule, the Spanish cruelly and single-mindedly looked for gold. When the Inca cities and tombs had been emptied, the Spanish opened mines to get mercury and more silver. The laborers were essentially slaves, and many did not survive the working conditions they endured. There were occasional uprisings against the Spanish, but none succeeded, and the result was often harsher working conditions.

Independence fever swept through Latin America in the early 1800s. Many countries fought for and gained their freedom after more than 200 years of Spanish control. Two outsiders brought independence to Peru. Argentine José de San Martín and Venezuelan Simón Bolívar had both successfully fought the Spanish to free their own countries. San Martín subdued the Spanish in Lima and declared independence for Peru on July 28, 1821. Bolívar would take over later and be president for two years.

Independence brought the early history of Peru to an end, but the decades that followed were not peaceful as Peru struggled to organize a nation.

Hiram Bingham, Explorer

You might be surprised to know that the Lost City of the Inca was never lost at all. Around the turn of the twentieth century, explorers and archaeologists searched Peru for Vilcabamba, the city mentioned in historical records as the last outpost of the Inca. A remnant of the Inca people had held out there against the Spanish conquistadores for over thirty years after Cuzco, the main Inca city, fell.

Hiram Bingham, who liked to be called an explorer rather than a scholar, came to Peru to search for the Lost City. The day he made his great discovery, his companion explorers had stayed in their camp to mend clothes and collect butterfly specimens. The young explorer convinced a local to guide him and his guard, Sergeant Carrasco, up the mountain to look at some reported ruins. After a difficult trek, the guide opted to stay at the mountainside home of some friends while Bingham and the sergeant continued the climb.

Bingham's guide at this point was a young Indian boy. Bingham doubted the wisdom of this difficult scramble through the underbrush and rocks until the boy urged the two men up a flight of stone steps.

Bingham later described what he saw in his book *Lost City of the Inca.* "Surprise followed surprise in bewildering succession. We came to a great stairway of large granite blocks. Then we walked along a path to a clearing where the Indians had planted a small vegetable garden. Suddenly we found ourselves standing in front of the ruins of two of the finest and most interesting structures in ancient America. Made of beautiful white granite, the walls contained blocks of Cyclopean size, higher than a man. The sight held me spellbound."

Bingham wasn't sure then or later if he had found Vilcabamba or some other Inca city that was unknown to historians. As it was proven many years later, he had found Machu Picchu, which would become one of the best-known and most spectacular of the Inca ruins. Vilcabamba turned out to be located much lower on another mountain. Neither site was "lost," but the indigenous people and the few other visitors hadn't attached particular importance to the ruins.

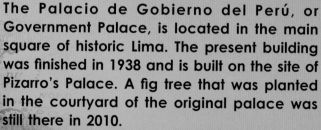

The Palacio de Gobierno del Perú, or Government Palace, is located in the main square of historic Lima. The present building was finished in 1938 and is built on the site of Pizarro's Palace. A fig tree that was planted in the courtyard of the original palace was still there in 2010.

Peru had thirty-five presidents between 1825 and 1865, showing the chaos that lingered long after the Spanish left. Many of these presidents were military men. It was 1872 before Peru's first civilian president, Manuel Pardo, was elected.

In 1879 Chile declared war on Peru and Bolivia over mineral deposits in Tarapacá province. Neither Peru nor Bolivia was prepared for war like Chile was. The War of the Pacific (1879–83) left Peru in ruins economically. Defeated, Peru was forced to give the disputed province to Chile in 1883.

In another longstanding dispute, Ecuador and Peru did not agree on their shared land border until 1998. They still dispute the sea boundary.

By the end of the nineteenth century, political parties representing different segments of Peru's society began to form. However, Peru's government and economy were still dominated by a small group of wealthy families and influenced by foreign interests.

The usual parade of presidents and military coups continued in Peru during most of the twentieth century. Economic and social progress was slow, with many setbacks.

In 1924, Victor Haya de la Torre formed a new political party, called the American Popular Revolutionary Alliance (APRA). This party championed the rights of the middle- and working-class people

Víctor Raúl Haya de la Torre

of Peru. APRA was active throughout the twentieth century but was largely kept out of power until the 1980s.

A military coup in 1968 made General Juan Velasco Alvarado president. Velasco instituted many social and economic reforms but landowners and businessmen opposed him. Worldwide price drops for sugar and copper, which Peru exported, led to unrest as the economy worsened. Velasco was replaced by another general in 1975.

Meanwhile highland guerrilla groups formed to fight the government. The two main guerrilla groups were the Sendero Luminoso, or Shining Path, which was communist-based, and Movimiento Revolucionario Tupac Amarú (MRTA), which was formed to gain a better life for the poor. Their numbers grew until the 1980s when civil war broke out.

The guerrillas used bombing, looting, kidnapping, and assassination to fight the Peruvian government. The army, police, and government death squads fought back fiercely. Because it was difficult to tell who the enemy was, many thousands of innocent people were killed. More than 3,000 people died in the violence in 1989 alone.

In the early 1990s, the leaders of both guerrilla groups were captured and the violence subsided. It seemed that the guerrilla threat was over until December 1996, when a group of MRTA guerrillas attacked the Japanese ambassador's home in Lima during a party. The MRTA took almost 500 people hostage. Many of them were released, but the incident wasn't brought to an end until April 1997. Peruvian troops attacked the home, and twelve rebels, two soldiers, and one hostage were killed.

Alberto Fujimori had been elected president in 1990. A Peruvian of Japanese descent, Fujimori made great headway with economic and social reform in Peru. However, as the years went by, he became increasingly authoritarian in his approach to the Peruvian Congress and governing in general.

It was the late 1990s before President Fujimori finally stopped the guerrilla groups. His methods often violated civil rights and led to outright abuse of citizens on both sides of the struggle. He also instituted drastic reforms to solve economic problems. Fujimori was successful in many of his efforts, but shortly after he began his third term in July 2000, a scandal broke that would prove to be his undoing.

Fujimori's close associate and adviser Vladimiro Montesinos had built a huge fortune for himself using bribery and other corrupt means. Videos of Montesinos

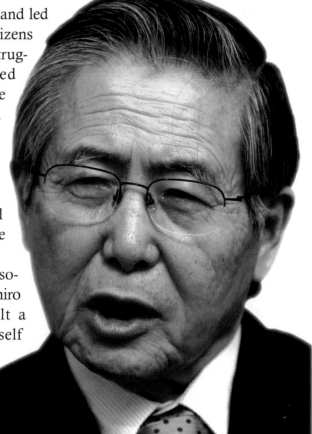

Alberto Fujimori

being bribed by a Peruvian official appeared on television, and Montesinos fled the country. Support for Fujimori evaporated.

In November 2000, Fujimori left Peru to attend an economic forum in Brunei. On the way home, he stopped in Tokyo, where he faxed his resignation to Lima. The Peruvian Congress refused to accept the resignation and instead impeached their president.

Fujimori was charged with numerous crimes but was not extradited from Japan. When he tried to make a comeback in 2005, he was arrested in Chile and returned to Peru to stand trial for corruption and human rights abuse charges. The last of his four trials on different charges ended in September 2009. He was convicted or pled guilty to all crimes and sentenced to several jail terms.

Fujimori is featured on a political poster titled *Se Busca* (Wanted).

In 2001, Peru appointed a Truth and Reconciliation Commission to investigate the crimes that occurred during the years of violence between the government and the guerrilla groups. The commission reported that 69,000 Peruvians had died as a result of the violence. Most were farmers and shepherds who had nothing to do with the guerrillas.

Alan García Pérez was elected president in 2006. He had been president before, from 1985 to 1990. His first term wasn't a successful one. He presided over hyperinflation in Peru's economy and also failed to combat the terrorists successfully. There were also allegations of official corruption. García was reelected in 2006 after he said he had learned from the mistakes of his first term. He promised to improve Peru's social condition with economic reforms and increased social spending.

When García was elected, seven different political parties won seats in Peru's unicameral Congress. There were another

Alan García Pérez

16 political parties that didn't win any of the 120 seats. The Congressional members are elected for five-year terms, as is the president. The president cannot be elected to consecutive terms, but he can run again after a break of five years.

Recent years have seen relative political stability and great economic growth in Peru. Peru's people have much to look forward to in the twenty-first century.

A capuchin monkey gives a tamarin monkey a lift in the Amazon rain forest of Peru. Capuchin monkeys are considered one of the most intelligent species of primates. They make and use tools while living in complex social groups.

Extreme Geography

One of Peru's great attractions is the exciting range of landscapes to be found there. Peru is the third largest country in South America; its greatest length from north to south is 1,225 miles (1,970 kilometers). It has an amazing amount of variety in its types of land, climate, animals, and plants. Scientists say that of 101 possible ecological zones in the world, Peru has 84 within its borders.

The mighty Amazon River begins high in the Andes as a small glacier-fed stream. Tributaries feed one into another, growing larger as they flow north. The Amazon eventually turns eastward and flows through Brazil until it empties into the Atlantic Ocean.

The Andes Mountains run like a backbone of Peru, with the Amazon rain forest sloping away to the east and the coastal desert to the west. Within the Andes range are several smaller ranges, such as Cordillera Blanca and Cordillera Occidental.

West of the Andes lies a narrow coastal desert with rivers that flow into the Pacific. The Peruvian capital, Lima, is located in this desert region. Lima sometimes receives less than 2 inches (5 centimeters) of rain in a year. The desert extends the full length of Peru—1,500 miles (2,400 kilometers) long and between 10 and 100 miles (16 and 160 kilometers) wide.

The Humboldt Current that occurs in the Pacific just off the coast of Peru helps maintain the coastal desert. The current is much colder than the usual coastal currents and causes a thermal inversion. Cooler air stays close to the surface, and higher air is warmer. The result can be dense fog but no rain. Lima has this fog for months of the year. In some coastal areas the fog is so thick that enough water condenses to allow plants to grow. These areas are called lomas.

The Andes rise abruptly east of the desert. Few people live above 14,000 feet (4,300 meters) in the mountains because of the ruggedness and lack of oxygen. Below that, Peruvians are farmers and shepherds. Crops grown depend on the altitude and the local terrain.

The eastern side of the Andes, called the selva, is divided into two parts. The high selva runs the length of the eastern side of the mountains and is called the eyebrow of the rain forest. Much of the land at this altitude is covered with cloud forests, which are areas of dense vegetation covered in mist and clouds most of the time.

The low selva is the huge rain forest of the Amazon Basin, with its thousands of plant and animal species. Although native plants and animals flourish there, the rain forest land is not good for farming. Only 12 percent of Peru's population lives in the Amazon Basin, even though the land area is 60 percent of the total area of Peru.

The caiman lives in the Amazon rain forest in Peru. It has powerful jaws that can crush other animals. This reptile is endangered because it has been hunted for its meat and hide.

Uros Indians in traditional dress get ready to launch their reed boat. The Uros build the boats from totora reeds that grow in Lake Titicaca. It takes more than a month to make a reed boat.

In southern Peru is the world's highest navigable lake. Around it, subsistence farmers grow potatoes and herd llamas and alpacas. Lake Titicaca is over 12,500 feet (3,800 meters) above sea level and is shared with Bolivia. This area between two of the southern mountain ranges, called an altiplano, is very rugged with cool temperatures. Legend says that the Inca originated in this area before moving farther north.

The climate of Peru is as variable as the terrain. The northern edge of Peru is right below the equator, which should mean that Peru has a hot, humid, equatorial climate. While the Amazon Basin has that climate, the rest of Peru has many climate zones that are far from tropical.

While it is quite dry on the coast, the temperatures are mild and average daily high temperatures vary less than 15°F (8°C) all year in Lima. The average summer high in February in Lima is 80°F (26°C), while the average winter high in July, August, and September is 66°F (19°C). The average low temperatures are always in the 60s (15 to 20°C).

The highland temperatures are almost solely determined by the altitude. In general the mountainous areas have cold, dry weather in winter (June, July, August) and are warmer with seasonal rains in the summer (January, February, March).

The Amazon low selva is always hot and humid. It rains year round, but the torrential rains that cause flooding and mudslides occur mainly from October through April. Average high temperatures are around 90°F (32°C), with average lows around 70°F (21°C) year round. These highs and lows vary only a few degrees in any season.

El Niño causes havoc with the weather every few years. This warm-water current sweeps from the equator into the cold waters of the Humboldt Current. It was first called the El Niño or "Christ Child" because fishermen observed it beginning around Christmas. El Niño causes torrential rains to fall in parts of Peru that seldom get any rain, such as the coastal desert. The flooding can be devastating to Peruvians

living along the coast and in the river valleys near the coast. The highlands also get more rain, but the southern edge of the selva may have droughts at the same time.

The coastal desert supports cacti and grasses that can survive in the arid conditions, but the river valleys that bisect the desert have plants unique to them. In areas on the coast where the seasonal fogs and mists provide moisture, deer, iguanas, skunks, and giant turtles can be seen. The coastal waters have sea lions, seabirds, and dozens of species of fish.

Above the tree line in the mountains only grasses such as ichu and some other drought-resistant bushes can grow. Lower down on the mountains, the plants become greener and more abundant. The highlands or sierra is home to alpacas, vicuñas, chinchillas, and other hardy mountain animals. Mosses, orchids, and bromeliads grow in the cloud forests of the high selva. The cloud forests support hummingbirds and the rare spectacled bear, while condors range throughout Peru but are seldom seen.

The Amazon rain forest is well known for its diversity of plants. More than 30,000 plant species alone are found there. One of the more spectacular is the Giant Amazon water lily (*Victoria amazonica*). The lily pad or leaf is four feet (1.2 meters) or more in diameter.

The rain forest is a jackpot of animals, birds, and insects. The giant river otter, giant anteater, sloth, spider monkey, and jaguar live there, along with macaws, parrots, piranhas, and thousands of other species, some of which are found only in the rain forest.

Aguas Calientes, also called Machupicchu Pueblo, is the closest town to the ancient Inca ruins of Machu Picchu. Trains run daily to and from the town from Cuzco and Ollantaytambo. Once here, tourists are about 4 miles (6 kilometers) from the magnificent ruins.

Peru's People

The people of Peru have a rich mixture of ethnic and national backgrounds, and it has been this way since Pizarro waded ashore in 1532. Unions between the Inca and their Spanish conquerors began almost immediately. Pizarro himself lived with two royal Inca princesses and had four children. Intermarriage continued as people immigrated from Europe and migrated within Peru.

Today in Peru, 37 percent of citizens are of mestizo or mixed background. Indigenous natives account for 45 percent of Peruvians. These native people live mostly in the Andes sierra and in the Amazon Basin. White or European Peruvians make up 15 percent of the population. The remaining 3 percent are of African, Japanese, Chinese, and other descent.

The largest numbers of mestizos live on the Pacific coast in urban areas and in other inland urban areas. The mestizo ranks can be swollen into a majority of Peruvians if the citizens who are mestizo by choice rather than birth are counted. In much of Peru's sierra, if you dress in western clothes, you are referred to as mestizo.

Peru has two official languages; Spanish and Quechua, which was the language of the Inca Empire. There are other more localized languages such as Aymara, and Quechua itself has several dialects. Quechua and other non-Spanish languages dominate the Andean highlands and the forests of the Amazon.

Scientists and researchers disagree about whether or not there are any uncontacted native groups or tribes in the mountains and jungles of central and eastern Peru. A true uncontacted tribe would be one that had never met Europeans or any other nationality outside of their Indian neighbors. It is not likely that there are any, but there are many tribes who do not maintain any regular contact with the outside world.

The Q'eros people and the Asháninka tribe are two examples of indigenous Peruvians who have rather recently been thrust into the modern world. The Q'eros live in the mountains of southeastern Peru and have kept their ancient traditions and beliefs to a much greater extent than most other indigenous Peruvians. In the rain forest of central Peru, the Asháninka people live much as they did centuries ago.

All of Peru's indigenous people suffered from the civil war in the 1990s between the government and the guerrillas. The forests and the highlands were the scenes of fierce fighting, and many native people were killed or displaced by both sides.

Catholicism came to Peru with Spanish conquistadores. As in all Spanish colonies, Catholic priests arrived almost immediately after conquest to convert the natives. Now, slightly more than 80 percent of Peruvians are Roman Catholic, although in recent years some Protestant groups have established congregations.

When they arrived, the priests took a practical approach to the native religions being practiced. They incorporated native rites when possible. They also built churches on top of Inca temples. In Cuzco, they built the magnificent Catedral on top of the palace of Inca Wiracocha. The altar there is made of solid silver.

Southeast of the Catedral in Cuzco is the Inca Temple of the Sun. The Spanish conquerors were astonished when they first saw it. The walls were covered in 700 sheets of gold studded with emeralds and turquoise, and the windows were built so that the sun would shine in and cast a blinding reflection off the gold. The Spanish built a church, Iglesia Santo Domingo, over this temple.

When nothing else worked, the Spanish intimidated the indigenous peoples into following Catholic practices. The result is a Peruvian society that continues to rest on Catholic values and principles. Religious practices and celebrations are deeply embedded in the everyday lives of most modern Peruvians.

Peruvians celebrate approximately 3,000 holidays and festivals every year. Most are local celebrations to honor a village or town's patron saint or perhaps to celebrate the founding day. Many of the national holidays have a religious origin, including all of the holidays surrounding Easter and Christmas.

Inti Raymi, the Festival of the Sun, is probably the best example of the combining of the two cultures. The weeklong celebration ends on June 24 with an elaborate ceremony in Cuzco. Hundreds of citizens dressed in traditional Inca costumes climb in a procession up to the ruins of Sacsayhuaman. Thousands of tourists from Peru and all over South America travel to Cuzco to watch the procession and the ceremonies enacted in the ruins.

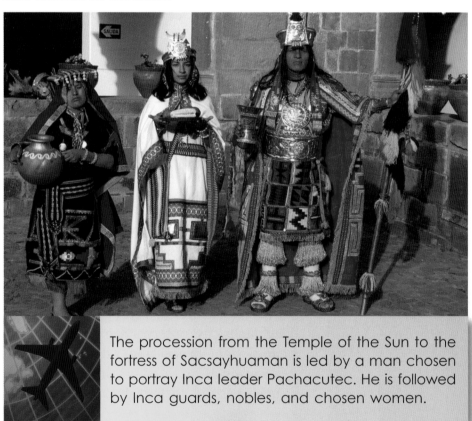

The procession from the Temple of the Sun to the fortress of Sacsayhuaman is led by a man chosen to portray Inca leader Pachacutec. He is followed by Inca guards, nobles, and chosen women.

The Inca observed Inti Raymi as a ceremony to convince the sun to return from its journey to the south. In Peru, the winter solstice is in June. Spanish priests managed to nudge the date of the celebration a few days forward to June 24 from the actual solstice day on June 21 so that Inti Raymi would fall on St. John the Baptist day. That way the priests could introduce a religious element to the already well-established and popular festival. Inti Raymi is celebrated with street fairs, dancing, free concerts, and reenactments of Inca ceremonies.

Carnival, the celebration that precedes the beginning of Lent, is celebrated with great enthusiasm in Peru. In some places the observance continues for a whole month rather than the week that is customary in most other countries. There are parades, fireworks, and street dances. The biggest Peruvian Carnival celebration takes place in Cajamarca in the Andes. Everyone dresses up, and some wear elaborate homemade costumes, which often have themes. Groups might wear white, purple, and lilac dresses to represent the different colors of potato flowers.

A well-known custom of Carnival in Peru involves water, and lots of it. Partygoers throw water balloons and shoot water guns at each other. The more adventurous people fling flour, ink, and oil "bombs" from their vehicles along with the water balloons. Nearly everyone enjoys getting soaked during Carnival in Peru.

Semana Santa, or Holy Week, is the week before Easter. Festivals surrounding Easter are sometimes religious, but as it is the last long weekend of the summer, many Peruvians go to the beach or otherwise get away for a break. Ayacucho, a central highlands city, observes Semana Santa with candlelight processions, daily fairs, and flower-petal artwork on the streets. Ayacucho has the greatest density of churches

FYI FACT:

A popular rice and fish soup in Peru, *aguadito*, is supposed to have restorative powers. It was traditionally served after the three-day wedding celebrations that were once common on Peru's coast.

Devil Dancers in Puno celebrate the folklore festival Virgen de la Candelaria.

of any Peruvian city, which might partly explain the exuberant Easter celebration.

Another popular festival is the Virgen de la Candelaria. It is celebrated throughout the Andes highlands, but the city of Puno lays claim to the biggest and best celebration. The festival takes place over 18 days around the beginning of February and combines religious ceremonies and events with a huge dance competition. Hundreds of musical and dance groups from all around the Lake Titicaca area come to Puno to compete. Many different ethnic dances are performed, but the most famous is the Diablada or Devil Dance. Devil Dancers wear grotesque masks and enact a legend related to a long-ago mining accident, when the Virgen de la Candelaria rescued some trapped miners.

Peruvians celebrate Labor Day on May 1 and Independence Day on July 27 through July 29. October 8 brings a holiday to commemorate the Grand Admiral Miguel Grau. He fought bravely from his ship *Huáscar* at the Battle of Angamos in 1879 during the War of the Pacific with Chile.

The people of Peru love a good celebration, and their government has made sure that they have many holidays to do just that.

Totora reed fishing boats are left upright to dry on the beach at Huanchaco near Trujillo. The fishermen here have been using these boats since ancient times. A skilled fisherman can construct one of these boats in an hour.

Chapter

5

Jobs
in Peru

The basis for Peru's economy has long been its natural resources, providing jobs in mining, agriculture, and fishing. The economy still rests mainly on the export of these resources, but industry, services, and technology have also contributed to Peru's healthy economy. It has continued to grow even through the worldwide economic downturn that began in late 2007.

One of Peru's first economic booms came mid-nineteenth century from a natural resource—bird poop. Seabird droppings on small islands off the southwest coast of Peru are called guano (which is Quechua for "the droppings of seabirds"). Long before the Inca ruled Peru, seabird poop was used to fertilize plants.

European colonists realized the importance of guano to increase crop production and soon began exporting it, particularly to England. Laborers worked on the islands and nearby rocky shores to scoop up the layers of guano that had collected there for centuries. (Many workers became sick and died from breathing the ammonia fumes.) The guano was shipped to Europe and America, where it sold for a handsome profit.

The development of cheaper chemical fertilizers and the depletion of the guano supplies caused the guano boom to bust by 1880. The Peruvian government had not foreseen these developments and had recklessly invested and spent the profits from the guano trade. The economy took a strong hit from this lack of foresight.

A lesser economic boom for Peru came about after a method to vulcanize rubber was invented. Rubber had been used since well before Columbus arrived in the New World, where he saw natives playing with hard rubber balls made from the sap of a rubber tree. The rubber was sticky at high temperatures and rock-hard at low ones. If temperatures were high enough, the rubber deteriorated into a gooey mess. Peru's Amazon rain forest had many rubber trees, particularly in the area around Iquitos.

Charles Goodyear discovered in 1838 that if he heated the raw rubber with sulfur, he could make a strong, stable product that held its shape and elasticity in any temperature. The rubber boom in Peru began in the 1880s and continued until around 1912. The rubber trade collapsed because American and European companies began planting rubber tree plantations in Asia, where the rubber could be more cheaply produced.

In most of Peru, farming is a difficult business, with the rough terrain and lack of water. The *ceja de selva,* or "eyebrow of the rain

Residents of Taquile Island in Lake Titicaca make their living from farming, fishing, and tourism. Taquile men knit the distinctive colored hats called *chullos* that they wear and sell to tourists. The colors and designs on the hats tell whether or not a man is married and if he has public authority.

Coffee beans are the seeds found inside coffee berries, which are often called coffee cherries. When the berries turn red, they are ripe and ready to be picked.

forest," is one of the more attractive areas for agriculture. Coffee and many tropical fruits are grown there. In the past it has also grown much of the world's coca crop. The leaves of the coca plant are used to produce cocaine, an illegal and dangerous drug that has caused a myriad of problems worldwide. Peruvians and other South Americans have chewed coca leaves for hundreds of years. The leaves were not processed into cocaine, but were used to provide energy and ward off hunger and thirst.

Potatoes are king in much of the Andean highlands. Over 3,000 varieties of potatoes are grown in Peru. The highlanders raise llamas, sheep, and alpacas for their wool. Pigs, goats, and guinea pigs are raised for food and milk.

Irrigation helps many of the warmer mountain valleys and coastal desert areas produce more food. The Inca and other indigenous peoples devised sophisticated irrigation systems to grow much more food for their people than could otherwise have been produced.

Commercial fishing is an important source of income. The Humboldt Current supports a rich variety of tiny sea creatures called plankton that larger fish eat. Peruvian coastal fish include swordfish, marlin, giant squid, mahimahi, and sea bass. Anchovies and other fish

On the hills above Urubamba in the Sacred Valley lie the Inca salt pans. Used since ancient times, the salt pans are hundreds of shallow pools. A salty spring was routed to fill the many pools. The hot sun evaporates the water, and the resulting salt is harvested.

FYI FACT:

After potatoes are harvested in the Andean highlands, they are spread out on the ground and left to freeze during the night. The next day after the sun thaws the potatoes, the farmers trample on them barefoot to squeeze out as much moisture as possible. This process is repeated for two or three nights until the potatoes are dry and ready to be stored. When needed, the dried potatoes can be rehydrated with any liquid.

are also used to make fish meal, which is exported to the United States and other countries.

The service industries in Peru employ the vast majority of Peruvians—over 75 percent. Service industries include any kind of work that does not produce a specific item. Tourism, banking, and shipping are examples of service industries.

There is also a smaller manufacturing or industrial segment in such areas as metal fabrication, mining and refining of minerals, textiles, clothing, and food processing. This group is still much larger than the one percent of Peruvians employed in agriculture.

Peru's unemployment rate is no higher than that of most other countries around the world, but a great many of Peru's poor, particularly in cities, are classified as underemployed. These people work as vendors on street corners and at markets, selling food, clothing, shoes, and other dry goods. They also may offer services right on the street, including cutting hair, mending torn clothes, shining shoes, or washing cars. Taxis are abundant in Lima—anyone with a car can put a sign on his windshield advertising his services.

Peru is not a country of rich people by any measurement. While nearly 40 percent of Peruvians still live with incomes that are below the poverty level, leaders in Peru feel that this number can be lowered over the next few years.

Anywhere there is a flat space in Peru, be it green grass or gravel, a soccer game may be in progress. Out-of-bounds in the mountains may be up a mountainside or over the side of a steep cliff.

Sports, Music, and Food

Peru is soccer crazy. Almost everyone in the country watches soccer, talks about soccer, and knows what Peru's chances are to qualify for the FIFA World Cup every four years. There are soccer fields in the mountains, in deserts, and in clearings in the rain forest. There are school teams from primary through university. Children play in the streets and adults play in the parks.

Lima has two teams that share most of the glory and rivalry for national soccer. Alianza has been a mostly Afro-Peruvian team drawing its support from working-class soccer fans, while Universitario appeals to upper-class mestizos. Supporters of the two teams have a bitter rivalry that extends beyond Lima. There are other national teams, but most Peruvians stand solidly behind Alianza or Universitario.

Another popular sport in Peru is women's volleyball. The Peruvian team has been a major competitor in regional and international play for several decades. They won a silver medal at the Seoul Olympics in 1988 and have placed highly in many international events since then.

Bullfighting and horseracing are also popular in Peru, as are many of the adventure sports such as surfing, mountain biking, rock climbing, and whitewater rafting. Sport fishermen have their choice of saltwater fishing on the coast, freshwater fishing in the Amazon, or trout fishing in the highlands.

The arts in Peru have been enriched by ballet companies and orchestras in Lima as well as by an array of art museums, but the primary expression of performing art in Peru still focuses on traditional dance and music. Every festival or party in Peru is an occasion to dance and sing or play instruments.

Music in Peru has its roots in ancient times. Wind instruments found in grave sites include flutes and panpipes of various sizes and styles. The flutes and panpipes produced haunting melodies and joined in complex duets. The Inca played conch-shell trumpets and drums made from the hides of Andean pumas.

The Spanish introduced stringed instruments, which were soon adopted by native musicians. The charango is a small mandolin made from the shell of the armadillo. Musicians use *tambors* or *bombas* for percussion. These are simple drums covered with hide and played with a stick.

These instruments provide the background for Peruvian dances. Some of the most popular dances include the *marinera*, the national dance of Peru. It is a formal dance of couples with much handkerchief fluttering and predetermined moves. A favorite group dance is the *kashua*, which is usually danced in the country or open spaces. The *huaylas* has energetic stomping while the *llamerada* imitates the llama's walk.

Peru has a rich history of handicrafts. Long before the Inca reigned, Peruvians were

Marinera dancers

making fine ceramics, weaving beautiful tapestries, and crafting metal objects. Bright colors are a hallmark of their handicrafts. Tourists are happy to pay for the dozens of items sold in markets. These sales provide an important income for many rural Peruvians.

Family events such as birthdays are celebrated in fine style, with the extended family and many friends attending. Food is an important part of every event. Families living near the coast would almost certainly serve *cerviche,* which is raw white fish marinated in lemon juice, onions, and hot peppers.

Fish might also be on the menu, with rainbow trout in the highlands and arapaima or even piranha in the Amazon region. In the high Andes and around Lake Titicaca, potatoes would be on the table as *papa a la huancaína,* a creamy mixture of potatoes, peppers, and boiled eggs, or as *papas rellenas,* which are potatoes stuffed with meat, onions, boiled eggs, and raisins. Hot peppers are used in a great many Peruvian dishes.

There is much less leisure time in Andean and Amazon Basin villages and among the poor in the coastal areas. They usually work from dawn to dusk every day just to feed their families. Even so, there are endless festivals to celebrate, and these events are also centered on family. Meanwhile, everywhere in Peru there is opportunity for the occasional soccer game in a nearby park or field.

Outspoken Peruvian writer Clorinda Matto de Turner wrote openly of the poor way that indigenous Peruvians were treated. She angered so many people that in 1895 her magazine printing business was raided and the equipment destroyed.

Famous Peruvians

Peru has produced many courageous and talented people since its early days. These individuals are just a few of many Peruvians who have inspired or entertained people around the world.

Clorinda Matto de Turner

Clorinda Matto de Turner was a controversial Peruvian writer in the late nineteenth century. She was born and grew up in Cuzco, Peru; her family was wealthy and sent her to a progressive school when she was a teenager. Her unconventional life began when she took classes there that were not considered feminine. She took courses such as philosophy, natural history, and physics.

After marrying a wealthy Englishman, Dr. José Turner, she and her new husband moved to Tinta. There she studied colonial and Inca history and began to write articles and stories in support of the indigenous peoples of Peru. It was not a popular viewpoint at the time, so her writing attracted attention both because she was a woman and because of its content.

By 1886, Matto had moved to Lima and begun to write novels with a political theme. The novels detailed the ways in which indigenous people were refused their civil rights and were often persecuted by the community and the priests. Because of these controversial novels, she was excommunicated from the Catholic Church by the archbishop in Lima.

Teófilo Cubillas

In 1895 the Peruvian president forced her to go into exile in Argentina. Matto continued to write, and these essays and articles reflected her sorrow over being exiled from her homeland. She often gave lectures and taught at a local university in Buenos Aires. She died in 1909.

Teófilo Cubillas

Teófilo Cubillas is considered the greatest soccer player in Peruvian history. Born in Puente Piedra in 1949, he began his career at age seventeen when he joined Alianza Lima, one of Peru's leading soccer clubs. He was his league's leading scorer in his first season.

Cubillas played in the 1970 World Cup tournament in Mexico, where he scored five goals in four games. In 1972 he was named South American Footballer of the Year. He played in Europe for a few years before returning to Peru. He played in his second World Cup in 1978 and was the second highest scorer with five goals.

After his World Cup success, Cubillas moved to the United States to play in the North American Soccer League. He achieved a career total of 892 matches, in which he scored 515 goals.

Cubillas retired in 1985 but made a brief return in 1987 after the entire Alianza Lima team was killed in a plane crash. Cubillas played to show respect for the fallen players and to give hope to the many soccer fans in Peru.

After retiring again in 1989, Cubillas settled in Coral Springs, Florida, where he teaches young players the art of playing soccer.

Tupac Amarú II

Tupac Amarú II was born José Gabriel Condorcanqui Noguera in the province of Cuzco in 1742. He was a mestizo and a direct descendent of the last Incan ruler, Tupac Amarú. The boy was educated at a Jesuit school in Cuzco, where he learned to read Latin and speak Spanish.

Condorcanqui became a wealthy businessman who respected the old Inca ways but went along with the Spanish colonial system. He became the chief of Tungasuca and Pampamarca when his older brother, the former chief, died. Gradually he became more and more disillusioned with the Spanish method of *mita*. He called for changes but was ignored.

The local Spanish governor, Antonio de Arriaga, was particularly cruel to the Indians. In a treasonous act to help his people, Condorcanqui had the governor executed. After he changed his name to Tupac Amarú II to reflect his support of the ancient Incan ways, he led a revolt that began in 1780.

There had been many uprisings against the Spanish but this one had more support than the others. Tupac Amarú II was an effective leader and attracted thousands of followers, but in the end he did not have enough support among the entire Peruvian native population. After several battles and skirmishes in which the Spanish were defeated,

Tupac Amarú II

the Spanish military finally got organized and captured Tupac Amarú II, his captains, and his family. They were executed, and the insurrection ended. In spite of Tupac's failure, he became an inspiration to later generations who struggled for freedom against the Spanish.

Susana Baca

Susana Baca was born in an African/Peruvian neighborhood in Chorrillos near Lima in 1944. Descendents of African slaves, her parents introduced her early to the music that reflected their background. At that time, Afro-Peruvian music was ignored by the mainstream culture in Peru. As a student Baca began researching her musical heritage and used that research to provide material for her part-time career as a professional singer.

For many years Baca and her husband, Ricardo Pereira, traveled throughout Peru, collecting and saving traditional folk music, which she then reinterpreted in her own performances. Younger artists began looking to her music as inspiration for their own.

Baca's big break arrived in 1995 when her song "Maria Lando" was included in an album called *The Soul of Black Peru,* which was a compilation of Afro-Peruvian songs. In 1997, her first solo album was released, and she has released a new album every two or three years since then. Baca won the Latin Grammy Award for Best Folk Album in 2002 for her *Lamento Negro* (Black Lament) CD. Her album *Seis Poemas* (Six Poems) was released in summer 2009.

Susana Baca

Highland Peruvians take good care of their animals. This baby llama, or *cria*, is very gentle and likes the attention his friend gives him. A cria weighs between 20 and 30 pounds (9 and 14 kilograms) at birth and is up and nursing within 90 minutes after birth.

Visiting Peru

Most visitors to Peru will start in Lima. Founded by Francisco Pizarro in 1535, the city originally had a grid of thirteen streets built on the site of an existing Indian settlement. During the city's first 200 years, it was the center of power for Spanish South America. Many of Lima's old buildings are from that colonial period, although most have been rebuilt after numerous earthquakes. One of them, the Monasterio de San Francisco, was built soon after Lima was established, but has suffered earthquake damage many times in the centuries since. Inside it has been restored to its original geometrical style and has a seventeenth-century library plus old murals and paintings. It also has underground chambers or catacombs, which were Lima's cemetery until 1810. They contain hundreds of skulls and bones stored on racks according to type.

Lima's Plaza Mayor is at the center of its historical district. The square is lined with rebuilt and renovated colonial buildings such as the Catedral, which was built on a site selected by Pizarro. Like the Monasterio de San Francisco, the Catedral has been repaired and reconstructed several times after earthquakes damaged or destroyed it. Pizarro's bones lie in a wooden coffin in a small chapel within the austere Catedral.

Next to the Catedral is the Palacio del Arzobispo, or Archbishop's Palace, and next to that is the Lima City Hall. The Palacio de Gobierno or Government Palace is also on the plaza; there's a "secret" passage from there to the Monasterio de San Francisco. The Government

In Lima's Circuito Mágico del Agua, there is a water tunnel through which visitors can walk and remain relatively dry. They can also walk through a fountain with timed water spouts to dodge.

Palace is built on the site of Pizarro's palace, where he was assassinated in 1541. Lima's attractions aren't all old buildings. The Circuito Mágico del Agua has thirteen fountains that display music, water, and light. There's also a water tunnel through which visitors can walk, fine restaurants, and shopping malls.

There are several markets and small shopping districts in Lima where a visitor can buy handcrafted products from all over Peru. These items range from gold- and silver-rimmed goblets to rain-forest blowpipes, woven alpaca garments, and tapestries.

The most famous sight to see in Peru is Machu Picchu. This magnificent Inca city was carved out of a mountaintop northeast of Cuzco. There are many theories about what kind of city Machu Picchu was. While the terraces used for farming were vast near the city, it appears that as few as 1,000 people made their homes in the city. It may have been a religious and ceremonial site. Most scholars agree that Machu Picchu was likely built, occupied, and abandoned in less than 100 years. Visitors to Machu Picchu come by train from Cuzco or on foot along the famous Inca Trail.

Lake Titicaca is also a popular destination, but visitors risk altitude sickness if they undertake strenuous activities. Legend says that the Inca civilization started at Lake Titicaca, and there is also evidence of inhabitants long before the Inca. A legend about the Uro people, who continue to live on the lake, says that they fled the aggressive Inca and settled on handmade totora reed islands that floated in Lake Titicaca. Today there are around 40 of these islands tethered in the lake. The Uros make the islands by harvesting totora reeds, which grow abundantly in the lake. The reeds are tied together to form bundles, which are then bound together to form small floating islands.

The reeds on the bottom of the islands rot away and are replaced on the top about every three months. It can take up to a year to

Totora reed islands that float on Lake Titicaca can be untied and floated to a new location if the residents desire. The surface of the islands feels squishy and is not easy to walk on until a person becomes used to it.

In northern Peru the city of Cajamarca is home to the Baños del Inca, the Inca baths. The city claims that it was in these hot springs that the Emperor Atahualpa bathed with his family. At their source, the springs are so hot that local people sometimes boil eggs in them.

construct a new island, and the islands last about thirty years. The Uros also construct elaborate reed boats to travel among islands and to the mainland.

The mysterious Nazca Lines are a popular tourist destination on Peru's southern coast. The lines lie on the pampa or plain north of Nazca, a small city that became famous about eighty years ago, when Paul Kosok, an American scientist, flew over Nazca in a small plane. He spotted the huge drawings, and the search for their origin began.

A German mathematician, Maria Reiche, spent fifty years studying the Nazca Lines and concluded that the lines and drawings were related to the constellations as part of a huge astronomical calendar. A more spectacular theory was put forth by Erich von Däniken, who argued that the lines were a giant landing strip for extraterrestrials.

With its diverse wildlife and plants, Parque Nacional Manú is one of Peru's greatest treasures. Located in the southeast part of Peru, this national park extends from the Andean highlands to the Amazon Basin. Closely protected, Manú contains one of the most pristine areas of rain forest in the tropics. Visitors must have permits to enter the reserve. Most tourists travel with a group because of its isolated location. It can take a couple of days to reach the main part of the park unless they come by small plane.

Bird watching in Manú is especially rewarding, since there are around 1,000 species of birds to be found. There are 13 species of monkeys and over 1,300 species of butterflies. Visitors have to watch out for crocodiles and caimans, since there are almost 100 species of reptiles.

Peru's attraction is easy to understand, with its colorful history, friendly people, and variety of places to see and things to do. It is at the top of many people's lists of places to visit.

Tacu Tacu

Tacu tacu has many variations and is often topped with steak or a fried egg.

3 cups mashed kidney beans
2 cups cooked rice
1 small red onion
1 fresh chili or jalapeño pepper
4 tablespoons vegetable oil
½ cup diced tomatoes
½ teaspoon salt (or more to taste)
⅛ teaspoon pepper (or more to taste)

Mix the mashed kidney beans with the rice in a deep bowl. Wearing latex gloves, chop or thinly slice the onion and pepper. DO NOT PUT YOUR HANDS TO YOUR EYES WHILE HANDLING THE PEPPER. **Under adult supervision,** heat the oil in a medium skillet until hot. Cook the onion and pepper in the oil until the onion is golden, about 3 to 5 minutes. Stir often. Add the tomatoes, salt, and pepper, and stir until the mixture is blended. Add the kidney beans and rice to the pan and stir until well mixed. Add more salt and pepper if desired. Reduce heat to medium and flatten the mixture into the skillet. Allow this to brown for 2 to 3 minutes on one side. Turn the *tacu tacu* onto a plate so that the brown side is up.

Tips:
Use a potato masher or ricer to mash the kidney beans.
Throw the gloves away and wash your hands thoroughly with soap after handling the pepper and onion.
Use red or green peppers in place of the chili or jalapeño peppers if you want less spiciness.
You can use fresh or canned tomatoes.
Four hands are better than two when turning the *tacu tacu* onto a serving plate. Put the plate upside down on top of the *tacu tacu* and flip the skillet. The *tacu tacu* should slip easily out of the pan.

Inca Water Jar Replica

You will need:
Air-drying clay
Cutting board
Rolling pin
Water in small container
Acrylic paints—black and brick red
Artist paintbrushes; a one-inch and a smaller one

1. Roll out a piece of clay on the cutting board. Make a circle that is about 6 inches in diameter and ½ inch thick.
2. Roll out clay snakes about as thick as your little finger. Using water as glue, dampen the edge of the pot bottom and coil a snake around the edge.
3. Coil more clay snakes on top of each other. Use your fingers to dampen the snakes to make them stick. Make each coil slightly smaller than the one below. Smooth the coils with your damp fingers. Don't push down hard to smooth, or the jar will collapse.
4. When you reach the neck of the jar, make several snakes the same length for two or three inches. Then place two slightly bigger coils to make a lip for the jar.
5. Use two more snakes to make handles on opposite sides of the jar. Use damp fingers to smooth out the seams carefully so that the handles will stay in place.
6. Let the clay dry completely. Paint the jar all over with the brick red paint.
7. After the red paint dries, use a small paintbrush to draw black Inca designs on the jar.

Tips:
Air-drying clay is recommended because it is easy to work with, but it is not waterproof. For a watertight jar, use real clay that is cooked in a kiln or oven.
The clay will be hard to work with at first but will soften as you handle it.
Add a tiny amount of water if the clay seems too dry.
Water is like glue for this kind of clay, but too much will dissolve the clay.
You can speed up the drying process by placing the jar in an oven that has been warmed to 200°F (90°C) and then turned off, or you can use a fan to dry the jar. Ask an adult to help with the oven.

TIMELINE

BCE

12,000   People live in Pikimachay (Flea Cave) near Ayacucho.

3000   First settlers live in river valleys on Peru's western coast.

1800   Monuments built with stone blocks appear.

900   Chavín culture is at its peak in highlands.

200   Nazca culture gains control of southern coast; they will flourish until about 700 CE. Nazca Lines are drawn.

CE

100–800   Moche culture rules northern coast.

550–950   Tiahuanaco Empire near Lake Titicaca is at its height of power.

850–900   Chimú capital city Chan Chan is built.

1200–1400   Incas rise to power.

1400–1500   Inca Empire expands throughout Peru.

1525   Death of Inca Huayna Capac starts Inca civil war.

1532   Francisco Pizarro arrives in Peru; conquest of Peru begins.

1535   Pizarro founds Lima.

1541   Pizarro is assassinated in Lima.

1572   Tupac Amarú, last Inca emperor, is executed; conquest is complete.

1780   Tupac Amarú II leads failed revolt against Spanish.

1821   Peru declares independence.

1850   Guano export gives Peru an economic boost.

1879–83   Peru sides with Bolivia against Chile in the War of the Pacific. Chile is victorious.

1880s   Rubber boom begins.

1911   Hiram Bingham discovers Machu Picchu ruins.

1924   Victor Haya de la Torre founds APRA political party.

1955   Women gain the right to vote.

1968   Military coup makes General Juan Velasco Alvarado president.

1980–92   Reign of terror by guerrilla groups Shining Path and MRTA.

1990   Alberto Fujimori is elected president.

1996   Japanese ambassador's home in Lima is under siege.

2000   Fujimori is forced to resign after scandal breaks.

2006   Alan García Pérez is elected president.

2009   U.S.–Peru Trade Promotion Agreement goes into effect.

2010   Paleontologists discover a 12-million-year-old fossilized whale skull in the Pisco-Ica Desert. It is a new species called *Leviathan melville*.

FURTHER READING

Books

Croy, Anita. *National Geographic Countries of the World: Peru.* Des Moines: National Geographic Children's Books, 2009.

Gruber, Beth. *Ancient Inca.* Washington D.C.: National Geographic Society, 2007.

Heaney, Christopher. *Cradle of Gold: The Story of Hiram Bingham, a Real-Life Indiana Jones, and the Search for Machu Picchu.* New York: Palgrave Macmillan, 2010.

Morrison, Marion. *Peru, Enchantment of the World.* New York: Children's Press, 2010.

Shields, Charles. *Peru (South America Today).* Broomall, PA: Mason Crest Publishers, 2009.

Sohn, Emily. *Investigating Machu Picchu: An Isabel Soto Archaeology Adventure.* Mankato, MN: Capstone Press, 2009.

Sonneborn, Liz. *Pizarro: Conqueror of the Mighty Inca.* Berkley Heights, NJ: Enslow, 2010.

Works Consulted

Baudin, Louis. *Daily Life in Peru.* New York: MacMillan, 1962.

Bingham, Hiram. *Lost City of the Inca.* New York: Atheneum, 1965.

Brown, Dale, Editor. *Inca: Lords of Gold and Glory.* Alexandria, VA: Time-Life Books, 1992.

Caistor, Nick. "Who Is Vladimiro Montesinos?" *BBC News,* November 22, 2000. http://news.bbc.co.uk/2/hi/americas/992770.stm

Davies, Nigel. *The Ancient Kingdoms of Peru.* New York: Penguin Books, 1997.

Descola, Jean. *Daily Life in Colonial Peru, 1710–1820.* New York: MacMillan, 1968.

Fagan, Brian, Editor. *Eyewitness to Discovery.* Oxford: Oxford University Press, 1996.

Hemming, John. *The Conquest of the Inca.* New York: Harcourt Brace Jovanovich, 1970.

Heyerdahl, Thor, Daniel Sandweiss, Alfredo Narvaez. *Pyramids of Tucumé: The Quest for Peru's Forgotten City.* New York: Thames and Hudson, 1995.

Holligan de Diaz-Limaco, Jane. *Peru: A Guide to the People, Politics, and Culture.* New York: Interlink Books, 1998.

Klaren, Peter Flindell. *Peru: Society and Nationhood in the Andes.* New York: Oxford University Press, 2000.

McIntyre, Loren. *The Incredible Inca and Their Timeless Land.* Washington, D.C.: The National Geographic Society, 1975.

MacQuarrie, Kim. *The Last Days of the Inca.* New York: Simon & Schuster, 2007.

Masterson, Daniel. *The History of Peru.* Westport, CT: Greenwood Press, 2009.

Parsell, D. L. "City Occupied by Inca Discovered on Andean Peak in Peru." *National Geographic News,* March 22, 2002. http://news.nationalgeographic.com/news/2002/03/0314_0318_vilcabamba.html

Starn, Orin, Carlos Ivan Degregori, Robin Kirk, editors. *The Peru Reader: History, Culture, Politics.* London: Duke University Press, 2005.

Wehner, Ross, and Renee del Gaudio. *Moon Handbooks: Peru.* Emeryville, CA: Avalon Travel Publishing, 2004.

On the Internet

CIA World Factbook: Peru
https://www.cia.gov/library/publications/the-world-factbook/geos/pe.html

Machu Picchu
http://www.peru-machu-picchu.com/

National Geographic: Peru Guide
http://travel.nationalgeographic.com/places/countries/country_peru.html

PBS: The Conquest of the Inca
http://www.pbs.org/conquistadors/pizarro/pizarro_flat.html

U.S. Department of State: Republic of Peru
http://www.state.gov/r/pa/ei/bgn/35762.htm

altiplano (al-tih-PLAY-noh)—A high plateau or plain of rolling grass, usually in the Andes Mountains.

authoritarian (ah-thar-ih-TAYR-ee-un)—Demanding unquestioned obedience.

bromeliad (broh-MEE-lee-ad)—A plant that usually grows on another plant and gets water and nutrients from the air and rain; they have stiff leathery leaves and spikes of bright flowers.

cloud forest—A forest that is high in a tropical mountain range and is covered by clouds or mists most of the time, including during the dry season.

conquistadores (kon-kee-stah-DOR-eez)—Spanish soldiers who conquered Mexico, Peru, and other Western Hemisphere countries in the sixteenth century.

Cyclopean (sy-KLOH-pee-un)—Huge or massive like the Cyclops race of giants in Greek mythology.

El Niño (el-NEE-nyoh)—A warm Pacific current that flows south annually around Christmas along the coast of Ecuador. Every seven to ten years, the current is stronger, causing weather disturbances off the coast of Peru.

excommunicate (eks-kuh-MYOO-nih-kayt)—To officially ban from the church.

extraterrestrial (ek-strah-ter-ES-tree-ul)—An object or creature that comes from outer space.

guerrilla (guh-RIH-luh)—A member of a small defensive force that makes surprise raids on enemies; also, war tactics that are used undercover to attack enemies.

Lent—The time period of forty days from Ash Wednesday to Easter, observed by Catholic churches.

mestizo/mestiza (mes-TEE-zoh/ -zah)—A person of mixed race, such as someone with one Spanish parent and one native Peruvian parent.

mita (MEE-tah)—A community tax paid in labor; laborers built public buildings and roads and provided other services for the upper class. Both the Inca and the Spanish used the *mita* system.

pampa (POM-pah)—A large treeless plain in South America.

reconciliation (reh-kun-sil-ee-AY-shun)—An agreement between two or more people or groups to become friendly again after a disagreement.

selva (SEL-vuh)—A tropical rainforest.

sierra (see-AYR-uh)—Highlands or mountainous areas.

unicameral (yoo-nih-KAM-uh-rul)—Having only one chamber, or group of lawmakers.

Alva, Walter   11
Alvarado, Juan Velasco   20
Amazon Basin   9, 26, 28, 31, 45, 57
Amazon rain forest   24, 26, 29, 38
Amazon River   25
American Popular Revolutionary
    Alliance (APRA)   19–20
Andes   14, 25–26, 31, 33, 34, 39, 45, 57
Atahualpa   16, 56
Ayacucho   34–35
Baca, Susana   50–51
Baños del Inca   56
Bingham, Hiram   17
Bolívar, Simón   16
Bolivia   14, 19, 27
Brazil   14, 25
Cajamarca   34, 56
Chavín   10
Chiclayo   11, 12
Chile   14, 19
Chimú   15
Colombia   14
Columbus, Christopher   38
Cubillas, Teófilo   48, 49
Cuzco   7, 11, 12, 17, 30, 32, 33, 47, 49,
    54
Ecuador   14, 19
Fujimori, Alberto   21–22
García Pérez, Alan   23
Goodyear, Charles   38
Government Palace   18, 53–54
Grau, Miguel   35
Haya de la Torre, Victor   19–20
Huayna Capac   16
Humboldt Current   25, 28, 39
Ica Desert   8
Inca   6, 9, 11, 14, 15, 16, 17, 27, 30, 31,
    32, 33, 34, 37, 39, 40, 44, 47, 49–50,
    54, 55, 56
Inca Wiracocha   32
Inti Raymi (Festival of the Sun)   33–34
Kosok, Paul   57
Lake Titicaca   12, 14, 27, 35, 38, 45, 55
Lima   9, 15, 16, 18, 21, 22, 25, 26, 28,
    41, 43, 47, 50, 53, 54
Machu Picchu   6, 7, 17, 30, 54–55

Matto de Turner, Clorinda   46, 47
Moche   6, 10–12
Movimiento Revolucionario Tupac Amarú
    (MRTA)   20–21, 32
Nazca Lines   6, 10, 57
Pachacutec   14, 33
Pardo, Manuel   19
Peru
    climate   13, 25–26, 28–29
    crops   9, 10, 12, 13, 20, 26, 38–39
    economy   19, 20, 23, 37–39, 40, 41
    festivals   33–35
    flag   13
    food   7, 34
    geography   8, 13, 25–29
    government   13, 18, 19–23
    history   9–12, 14–16, 17, 19–23
    immigration   7, 31
    language   13, 31, 37
    map   14
    music/dance   7, 9, 44, 50–51
    natural resources   13, 16, 20, 36,
        37–38
    religion   32–35, 47, 53
    sports   42, 43, 45, 48, 49
    wildlife   24, 29, 45
Pikimachay (Flea Cave)   9
Pizarro, Francisco   7, 16, 18, 31, 53
pyramids   6, 9, 12
Quiroga, Rámon   45
Reiche, Maria   57
Sacsayhuaman   33
salt pans   40
San Martín, José de   16
Sendero Luminosa (Shining Path)   20
Sicán culture   12
Sipán, Lord of   10–11
Temple of the Sun   32
totora reeds   27, 36, 55, 57
Tupac Amarú   20, 49
Tupac Amarú II   49–50
Uros   27, 55, 57
Vilcabamba   17
von Däniken, Erich   57
War of the Pacific   19, 35

Bonnie Hinman is the author of 20 books for young readers, including *The Pennsylvania Colony* and *We Visit Panama* for Mitchell Lane Publishers. Her biography of W.E.B Du Bois, *A Stranger in My Own House*, was selected for inclusion on the 2006 New York Public Library's Books for the Teen Age. Bonnie has been fascinated by the Inca ever since elementary school and was eager to find out more about Peru. She graduated from Missouri State University and lives in southwest Missouri with her husband, Bill. Her children and four grandchildren live nearby.